HARRY STYLES

A Little Golden Book® Biography

By Wendy Loggia

Illustrated by Ruth Burrows

The author dedicates this book to her son, Will: I adore you!
And her daughter: I love, love, love Olivia!

🌼 A GOLDEN BOOK • NEW YORK

Text copyright © 2024 by Wendy Loggia
Cover art and interior illustrations copyright © 2024 by Ruth Burrows
All rights reserved. Published in the United States by Golden Books, an imprint of
Random House Children's Books, a division of Penguin Random House LLC, 1745 Broadway,
New York, NY 10019. Golden Books, A Golden Book, A Little Golden Book, the G colophon,
and the distinctive gold spine are registered trademarks of Penguin Random House LLC.
rhcbooks.com
Educators and librarians, for a variety of teaching tools, visit us at RHTeachersLibrarians.com
Library of Congress Control Number: 2023951462
ISBN 978-0-593-71026-5 (trade) — ISBN 978-0-593-71027-2 (ebook)
Printed in the United States of America
10 9 8 7 6 5 4 3 2 1

Harry Edward Styles was born in England on February 1, 1994, to Desmond Styles and Anne Twist. His big sister, Gemma, was three years old when Harry arrived.

From the time he was a baby, Harry was full of mischief. The Styles family had a dog, Max. Sometimes little Harry would put his pacifier in Max's mouth!

Harry was fun to be around and made people happy. He was a good little brother, too. He played school with Gemma. She would be the teacher, and he would be the whole class. Harry used different voices for all the students.

Harry liked to entertain a crowd. His first performance was acting in a school play. Harry was a church mouse named Barney. He went on to sing in a school production of *Joseph and the Amazing Technicolor Dreamcoat*. The audience loved him. And Harry? He was hooked.

When Harry was a teenager, he worked at a local bakery. He liked serving cakes to customers. But Harry didn't want to be a baker. He wanted to be a rock star.

In high school, Harry and his friends were in a band called White Eskimo. Harry was the lead singer. They won a Battle of the Bands competition. Singing in front of so many people was thrilling. It made Harry realize how much he wanted to be a performer. And soon he'd have his big chance.

On April 11, 2010, Harry auditioned for the British television singing competition, *The X Factor.* Harry sang "Hey, Soul Sister." Judge Simon Cowell thought the background music was throwing Harry off. Luckily, he had prepared two songs!

So, Harry sang "Isn't She Lovely" next. One judge said Harry wasn't ready for the music business. But Simon and another judge disagreed. They sent him on to the next round—boot camp at London's Wembley Stadium!

All the performers at boot camp received vocal coaching and dance lessons. Harry was very upset when he didn't make it as a soloist in the Boys category. But then he was called back to the stage along with four other boys: Niall Horan, Liam Payne, Louis Tomlinson, and Zayn Malik. *The X Factor* judges said they could stay and compete on the show—as a group.

The boys called themselves One Direction. The band's name? That was Harry's idea! One Direction made it all the way to the finale and came in third place. After the show, Simon Cowell offered them a record deal. He knew they could be stars.

Soon, One Direction was famous everywhere! The band had a hit single, "What Makes You Beautiful." Their album, *Up All Night*, was a number one hit in America. Harry cowrote three of the songs.

One Direction made four more albums. They had millions of fans and toured around the world. But in 2016, the band decided it was time to take a break.

Being on his own might have been scary, but Harry was excited to be a solo artist. He believed in himself, kept trying new things, and became a worldwide superstar!

Harry's House won album of the year at the 2023 Grammy Awards. His Love on Tour concert sold out Madison Square Garden in New York City for fifteen nights in a row! A special banner was hung in the arena to celebrate. Harry was overwhelmed with gratitude.

Harry made his feature film debut in *Dunkirk*, playing a World War II soldier, and has continued to act in movies. He never had acting lessons, just the natural talent he discovered when he was in those school plays as a young boy. Harry said making *Dunkirk* was an amazing experience.

Everyone wants to hang out with Harry. He is friends with celebrities of all ages, including artists Stevie Nicks and Ed Sheeran. He is inspired by them—and has fun with them, too!

Harry isn't afraid to take risks and be himself.
Television host, movie star, songwriter, model—
Harry has done it all.

Something else Harry isn't afraid of? Tattoos!
He has over fifty! They include birds, a butterfly,
an anchor, and a ship. He got his first tattoo,
a star, on his eighteenth birthday.

Fashion and clothes have always been exciting for Harry. Now that he's a big star, he wears fancy custom-made suits, feather boas, even dresses. "There's so much joy to be had in playing with clothes," he has said. Harry's fashion choices inspire his fans, who dress up in bold colors and fantastic outfits at his concerts.

Even though he's one of the most famous people in the world, Harry takes the time to make people feel special. Once when his car broke down, Harry was invited inside a nearby house to wait for a tow truck and have a cup of tea. He was told that a girl who lived there was a big fan of Harry's, but she wasn't home. Harry left a sweet note for the girl—and a photo of him feeding her fish!

Treating People With Kindness—TPWK—is very important to Harry. He speaks out against hurtful behavior and supports the right for everyone to love who they love and be treated fairly.

MY CAR BROKE DOWN ON YOUR STREET AND YOUR DAD'S FRIEND KINDLY LET ME WAIT AT YOUR HOUSE WITH A CUP OF TEA. I'M DEVASTATED THAT WE MISSED EACH OTHER. LOOKING FORWARD TO MEETING YOU SOON. TREAT PEOPLE WITH KINDNESS.

ALL MY LOVE ♡ HARRY

P.S. I FED THE FISH.

TPWK

Harry Styles—the little boy who liked to make people smile—is still doing that as a grown-up. Through his music and his inclusive, positive energy, Harry helps make the world a happier place for his millions of fans!

It was Hap's birthday, but he wasn't celebrating. He was hard at work, answering questions as fast as the phones would ring. "Plutonium!" he snapped. "Sacagawea! Rin Tin Tin!"

Just then, Bing, Bang, Bo, Beep, and Boop rushed in, carrying a big cake and beautifully wrapped presents. "Happy birthday!" they shouted.

"Birthday?" Hap growled. "I don't have time for birthdays! There's work to do! What is a birthday, anyway? Just an excuse to dillydally?"

The StoryBots thought for a moment.
"What IS a birthday?" said Beep. "What
makes it special? We need to find out!"

Bo dashed to the keypad and punched
in a code. Down came the transport tubes.
"Outerworld, here we come!" the
StoryBots exclaimed.

The tubes dropped them in a hospital room. A baby girl was cooing in a bassinet while her mother slept nearby.

"Why did you bring us here?" Beep whispered.

"Well," said Bo, "a birth is when a baby is born. So who would know more about birthdays than a baby?"

"Hi, Emily!" said Bing. "Can you tell us about birthdays?"

Emily just stared and gurgled.

A nurse came in to check on the baby and her mother. "Well, hello, StoryBots," she said. "What brings you here?"

"We're, like, asking baby Emily about birthdays," said Bang. "Since she just had her birth, you know?"

"Emily hasn't actually had any birthdays yet," the nurse explained. "A birthday is the *anniversary* of someone's birth. She'll have her first birthday one year from today."

"But what's a year?" asked Bo.

"That's how long it takes to travel around the sun," said the nurse.

"Whoa, now I'm *really* confused!" said Bang. "But I know who can help."

"Thank you," they said to the nurse. "Bye, Emily!"

Soon they were in outer space. It was
hot and bright!

"Hello, StoryBots!" said the sun. "What
can I do for you?"

"We're trying to learn about birthdays,"
said Beep. "We heard it has something to
do with going around the sun."